1 & 2 PETER: OUR LIVING HOPE

HE READS TRUTH

HE READS TRUTH

EXECUTIVE

**FOUNDER /
CHIEF EXECUTIVE OFFICER**
Raechel Myers

**CO-FOUNDER /
CHIEF CONTENT OFFICER**
Amanda Bible Williams

**CHIEF OPERATING OFFICER /
CREATIVE DIRECTOR**
Ryan Myers

EXECUTIVE ASSISTANT
Catherine Cromer

EDITORIAL

CONTENT DIRECTOR
John Greco, MDiv

MANAGING EDITOR
Jessica Lamb

KIDS READ TRUTH EDITOR
Melanie Rainer, MATS

CONTENT EDITOR
Kara Gause

EDITORIAL ASSISTANT
Ellen Taylor

MARKETING

MARKETING MANAGER
Kayla Stinson

SOCIAL MEDIA STRATEGIST
Ansley Rushing

COMMUNITY SUPPORT SPECIALIST
Margot Williams

CREATIVE

ART DIRECTOR
Amanda Barnhart

DESIGNER
Kelsea Allen

ARTIST IN RESIDENCE
Emily Knapp

JUNIOR DESIGNER
Abbey Benson

SHIPPING & LOGISTICS

LOGISTICS MANAGER
Lauren Gloyne

SHIPPING MANAGER
Sydney Bess

FULFILLMENT COORDINATOR
Katy McKnight

FULFILLMENT SPECIALIST
Julia Rogers

SUBSCRIPTION INQUIRIES
orders@hereadstruth.com

COLOPHON

This book was printed offset in Nashville, Tennessee, on 60# Cream Lynx Opaque Text under the direction of He Reads Truth. The cover is 100# Cream Lynx Opaque Cover with a soft touch aqueous coating.

@hereadstruth   hereadstruth.com

Before returning to invent the iPhone and the iPad, Steve Jobs was fired from Apple. Before becoming president and presiding over a war-torn nation, Abraham Lincoln lost more elections than he won. Before becoming the most successful author of all time, J. K. Rowling was a single mom without a job, trying to make ends meet.

There's something great about a comeback story, isn't there? It's one of the reasons I love 1 and 2 Peter. Often slow to think and quick to act, Simon Peter was a man familiar with mistakes. But in these two short letters, we get a glimpse into the final chapters of his comeback.

The disciple who was afraid of what people might think, and so denied Jesus, now writes, "If you are ridiculed for the name of Christ, you are blessed" (1Pt 4:14; see Mk 14:66-72). The man who impetuously cut off a soldier's ear on the night Jesus was arrested now advises fellow believers, "Submit to every human authority because of the Lord" (1Pt 2:13; see Jn 18:10). The good friend whom Jesus charged with feeding His sheep is now a shepherd of shepherds (1Pt 5:2; see Jn 21:17).

Unlike most comeback stories, though, Peter's isn't a lesson in pulling up bootstraps or mustering some steely-eyed determination from deep within. His is a story about the grace of God and the power of the Holy Spirit. The hero of Peter's story isn't Peter; it's Jesus of Nazareth.

We called this reading plan *1 & 2 Peter: Our Living Hope*. The subtitle comes from 1 Peter 1:3, which says, in part:

> *Because of his great mercy he has given us new birth into a living hope through the resurrection of Jesus Christ from the dead.*

This "living hope" is the new life we now have with Christ and the future resurrection that is ours because we belong to Him. It's as sure as the law of gravity because of the salvation Jesus wrought for us on the cross. Our lives are being transformed into the greatest of comeback stories, at the end of which we will reign with the Lord forever as children of God—not because of anything we've done, but because of Jesus.

In this three-week Legacy Book, we've included some great resources to help you understand and reflect upon Peter's teaching. My prayer is that as you read, you will be encouraged by the same living hope that gave the recipients of these letters the courage to stand in the midst of persecution, so that whatever challenges you may be facing, you will see them framed in the light of eternity and God's great love for you.

For His kingdom,

JOHN GRECO
CONTENT DIRECTOR

When we create a new study book, we draw inspiration from a variety of (sometimes unusual) places. This vibrant fabric swatch from a men's dress shirt inspired the color palette for our 1 & 2 Peter book. Here, our creative director is reviewing the board our team put together with a cool blue and a bold red.

Each book in the He Reads Truth Legacy Series™ provides space to read and study Scripture, make notes, and record prayers. As you build your library, you will have a record of your Bible-reading journey to reference and pass down.

SCRIPTURE READING PLAN

Designed for a Monday start, this Legacy Book presents the books of 1 & 2 Peter in daily readings, with supplemental passages for additional context.

RESPONSE

Each daily reading closes with three reflection questions.

GRACE DAY

Use Saturdays to pray, rest, and reflect on what you've read.

WEEKLY TRUTH

Sundays are set aside for weekly Scripture memorization.

Find corresponding memory cards in the back of this book.

EXTRAS

This book features additional tools to help you gain a deeper understanding of the text.

1 & 2 Peter — 3 Weeks

PLAN OVERVIEW

The letters of 1 & 2 Peter were written to encourage believers in their faith. Peter's words are just as relevant to believers today as they were to his original readers in the first century. He reminds us that, as the people of God, we are called to a life of holiness and hope. Join us for this three-week plan as we study the books of 1 & 2 Peter, rich with the promise of our living, eternal hope in Christ.

For added community and conversation, join us in the **1 & 2 Peter** reading plan on the He Reads Truth™ app or at HeReadsTruth.com.

TABLE OF
CONTENTS

EXTRAS

PRINCIPLES FOR INTERPRETING SCRIPTURE	10
TIMELINE: 1 & 2 PETER IN HISTORY	12
THE PEOPLE OF GOD	26
MAP: PETER'S MINISTRY	52
HERESIES IN HISTORY	80
WHAT THE NEW TESTAMENT SAYS ABOUT FALSE TEACHING	82
FOR THE RECORD	104

WEEK

1

DAY 1	A Living Hope	17
DAY 2	A Call to Holy Living	23
DAY 3	A Holy People	28
DAY 4	A Call to Good Works	33
DAY 5	Wives and Husbands	37
DAY 6	Grace Day	40
DAY 7	Weekly Truth	42

WEEK

2

DAY 8	Do No Evil	44
DAY 9	Following Christ	49
DAY 10	Christian Suffering	55
DAY 11	About the Elders	59
DAY 12	Firm in the Faith	63
DAY 13	Grace Day	66
DAY 14	Weekly Truth	68

WEEK

3

DAY 15	Growth in the Faith	73
DAY 16	The Trustworthy Prophetic Word	77
DAY 17	The Judgment of False Teachers	85
DAY 18	The Day of the Lord	88
DAY 19	To Him Be the Glory	93
DAY 20	Grace Day	96
DAY 21	Weekly Truth	98

PRINCIPLES FOR INTERPRETING SCRIPTURE

How should we interpret what we read in the Bible? How should we approach passages that are hard to understand?

Every word of Scripture has a context. It belongs to a sentence, which belongs to a particular train of thought, which belongs to a book in a collection of sixty-six books called the Bible. As such, we must interpret the various parts of Scripture in light of the whole.

Practicing the art of interpreting Scripture is one of the great rewards of reading the Bible over the course of time. Here are some reminders and tips to help.

REMEMBER

The Bible was written for us, so that we might know God.
2TM 3:16-17

God does not change.
JMS 1:17

To truly understand Scripture, we need the Holy Spirit's help.
1CO 2:11

The gospel is simple enough for a child to understand and believe.
MK 10:13-15

God reveals truth progressively, but Christ is central to all of Scripture, from Genesis to Revelation.
JN 1:45

Scripture is meant to guide, convict, and change us.
HEB 4:12

The power and fruitfulness of Scripture is not dependent on us.
IS 55:11-12

Learning takes time.
PR 1:5

Doctrine can be complex; libraries are filled with books on theology.

PRACTICE

Begin with prayer, asking for the Holy Spirit's help.
JN 14:26

Interpret individual passages with the message of the whole Bible in view.
AC 17:11

Read the Old Testament with the New Testament in mind, and vice versa.
LK 24:27

Let the original application of a text inform its present application.
2PT 1:20-21

Interpret what is hard to understand in light of what is clearly taught.
2PT 3:16

Interpret using the ordinary rules of language and grammar.
JN 16:25

Interpret assuming Scripture is coherent and unified.
2CO 4:2

Interpret a passage according to its genre. For example: Isaiah as prophecy, Psalms as poetry, 1 Kings as history, Titus as a personal letter.

1 & 2 PETER IN HISTORY

AD 20

AD 29

● BIBLICAL EVENT

● EXTRABIBLICAL EVENT

Romans construct
Pont du Gard to
bring water to the
city of Nîmes

Peter's brother,
Andrew,
introduces him
to Jesus

Jesus calls Peter
to be the second
of His disciples

ca AD 1

AD 32

Birth of Simon
Peter in Galilee

Peter
confesses
that Jesus is
the Messiah,
and Jesus calls
Simon Peter
a name that
means "rock"

Peter, James,
and John
witness Jesus's
transfiguration

0   **10**   **20**   **30**

AD 33

Peter denies Jesus three times after vowing to die with Him

Following His resurrection, Jesus appears to Peter and recommissions him

3,000 people respond to Peter's sermon at Pentecost

AD 37

Peter and James meet with Paul on Paul's first visit to Jerusalem following his conversion

AD 40

Peter shares the gospel with Cornelius and his family at Caesarea Maritima

AD 43

The Roman emperor Claudius sends troops to conquer Britain

AD 49

Peter, James, John, Paul, Barnabas, and Titus meet at the Jerusalem Council to address the question of whether Gentiles must be circumcised to become Christians

AD 54

Nero becomes emperor of Rome

AD 62–64

1 Peter written

AD 66

2 Peter written

Peter's martyrdom in Rome

Jewish people in Judea revolt against Rome

AD 64

Great Fire of Rome causes wide destruction

40   50   60   70

HE HAS GIVEN US NEW·BIRTH INTO A LIVING·HOPE THROUGH THE RESURRECTION OF JESUS CHRIST

KEY VERSE
1 PETER 1:3-4

Blessed be the God and Father of our Lord Jesus Christ. Because of his great mercy he has given us new birth into a living hope through the resurrection of Jesus Christ from the dead and into an inheritance that is imperishable, undefiled, and unfading, kept in heaven for you.

ON THE TIMELINE

First Peter was likely written between AD 62 and 64, during the persecution of Christians under Nero's reign.

A LITTLE BACKGROUND

The author of 1 Peter identified himself as "Peter, an apostle of Jesus Christ" (1:1). He viewed himself as a divinely ordained, directly commissioned, authoritative representative of the Lord Jesus Himself. Several statements in the letter indicate that the Peter who plays a prominent role in the Gospels is the author. For example, he called himself an "elder and witness" to Christ's sufferings (5:1).

The recipients of 1 Peter are identified in 1:1. Peter wrote to "those chosen, living as exiles dispersed abroad in Pontus, Galatia, Cappadocia, Asia, and Bithynia." These were Roman provinces located in the northern part of what is now modern Turkey, unless "Galatia" includes the Galatia in the southern region of Asia Minor. These people were likely persecuted Gentile Christians. They had earlier been involved in idolatry (4:3), were ignorant and living a life of emptiness (1:14, 18) before they came to Christ, and formerly were "not a people" but now were "God's people" (2:9-10).

MESSAGE & PURPOSE

Peter wrote to encourage suffering believers in Asia Minor to stand firm for Christ in the midst of persecution. He did so by focusing on their spiritual privileges and the place where their rights and privileges truly lay: the next life. Believers in Jesus are "exiles" (1:1; 2:11) and "strangers" (2:11) in this world.

GIVE THANKS FOR THE BOOK OF 1 PETER

Peter's message of encouragement in the face of suffering continues to speak to believers today. First Peter reminds us of our heavenly hope and eternal inheritance. We are called to a life of love and holiness, glorifying God and imitating Christ in our daily lives.

...BECAUSE YOU ARE RECEIVING
THE GOAL OF YOUR FAITH, THE
SALVATION OF YOUR SOULS.

1 PETER 1:9

A LIVING HOPE

1 Peter 1:1-12
Exodus 24:3-8
Psalm 51

1 PETER 1:1–12

GREETING

¹ Peter, an apostle of Jesus Christ:

To those chosen, living as exiles dispersed abroad in Pontus, Galatia, Cappadocia, Asia, and Bithynia, chosen ² according to the foreknowledge of God the Father, through the sanctifying work of the Spirit, to be obedient and to be sprinkled with the blood of Jesus Christ.

May grace and peace be multiplied to you.

A LIVING HOPE

³ Blessed be the God and Father of our Lord Jesus Christ. Because of his great mercy he has given us new birth into a living hope through the resurrection of Jesus Christ from the dead ⁴ and into an inheritance that is imperishable, undefiled, and unfading, kept in heaven for you.

_____/_____/_____

DATE

[5] You are being guarded by God's power through faith for a salvation that is ready to be revealed in the last time. [6] You rejoice in this, even though now for a short time, if necessary, you suffer grief in various trials [7] so that the proven character of your faith—more valuable than gold which, though perishable, is refined by fire—may result in praise, glory, and honor at the revelation of Jesus Christ. [8] Though you have not seen him, you love him; though not seeing him now, you believe in him, and you rejoice with inexpressible and glorious joy, [9] because you are receiving the goal of your faith, the salvation of your souls.

[10] Concerning this salvation, the prophets, who prophesied about the grace that would come to you, searched and carefully investigated. [11] They inquired into what time or what circumstances the Spirit of Christ within them was indicating when he testified in advance to the sufferings of Christ and the glories that would follow. [12] It was revealed to them that they were not serving themselves but you. These things have now been announced to you through those who preached the gospel to you by the Holy Spirit sent from heaven—angels long to catch a glimpse of these things.

EXODUS 24:3–8

[3] Moses came and told the people all the commands of the LORD and all the ordinances. Then all the people responded with a single voice, "We will do everything that the LORD has commanded." [4] And Moses wrote down all the words of the LORD. He rose early the next morning and set up an altar and twelve pillars for the twelve tribes of Israel at the base of the mountain. [5] Then he sent out young Israelite men, and they offered burnt offerings and sacrificed bulls as fellowship offerings to the LORD. [6] Moses took half the blood and set it in basins; the other half of the blood he splattered on the altar. [7] He then took the covenant scroll and read it aloud to the people. They responded, "We will do and obey all that the LORD has commanded."

[8] Moses took the blood, splattered it on the people, and said, "This is the blood of the covenant that the LORD has made with you concerning all these words."

A PRAYER FOR RESTORATION

For the choir director. A psalm of David, when the prophet Nathan came to him after he had gone to Bathsheba.

¹ Be gracious to me, God,
according to your faithful love;
according to your abundant compassion,
blot out my rebellion.
² Completely wash away my guilt
and cleanse me from my sin.
³ For I am conscious of my rebellion,
and my sin is always before me.
⁴ Against you—you alone—I have sinned
and done this evil in your sight.
So you are right when you pass sentence;
you are blameless when you judge.
⁵ Indeed, I was guilty when I was born;
I was sinful when my mother conceived me.

⁶ Surely you desire integrity in the inner self,
and you teach me wisdom deep within.
⁷ Purify me with hyssop, and I will be clean;
wash me, and I will be whiter than snow.
⁸ Let me hear joy and gladness;
let the bones you have crushed rejoice.
⁹ Turn your face away from my sins
and blot out all my guilt.

¹⁰ God, create a clean heart for me
and renew a steadfast spirit within me.
¹¹ Do not banish me from your presence
or take your Holy Spirit from me.
¹² Restore the joy of your salvation to me,
and sustain me by giving me a willing spirit.
¹³ Then I will teach the rebellious your ways,
and sinners will return to you.

[14] Save me from the guilt of bloodshed, God—
God of my salvation—
and my tongue will sing of your righteousness.
[15] Lord, open my lips,
and my mouth will declare your praise.
[16] You do not want a sacrifice, or I would give it;
you are not pleased with a burnt offering.
[17] The sacrifice pleasing to God is a broken spirit.
You will not despise a broken and humbled heart, God.

[18] In your good pleasure, cause Zion to prosper;
build the walls of Jerusalem.
[19] Then you will delight in righteous sacrifices,
whole burnt offerings;
then bulls will be offered on your altar.

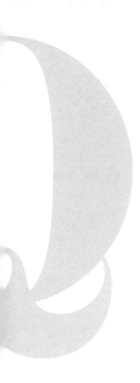

QUESTIONS
———

What did you notice about this passage?
What was your immediate reaction upon reading this passage? Did anything stand out to you?

What questions do you have?
Did anything in this passage confuse you? Are there any words or concepts you don't understand? What questions would you like to dig into further?

How will you respond?
What is the truth to be applied from this passage? How is God using this passage to teach you more about Him?

2

A CALL TO HOLY LIVING

1 Peter 1:13-25
Isaiah 53:7-9
Ephesians 1:3-10

1 PETER 1:13-25

A CALL TO HOLY LIVING

¹³ Therefore, with your minds ready for action, be sober-minded and set your hope completely on the grace to be brought to you at the revelation of Jesus Christ. ¹⁴ As obedient children, do not be conformed to the desires of your former ignorance. ¹⁵ But as the one who called you is holy, you also are to be holy in all your conduct; ¹⁶ for it is written, Be holy, because I am holy. ¹⁷ If you appeal to the Father who judges impartially according to each one's work, you are to conduct yourselves in reverence during your time living as strangers. ¹⁸ For you know that you were redeemed from your empty way of life inherited from your fathers, not with perishable things like silver or gold, ¹⁹ but with the precious blood of Christ, like that of an unblemished and spotless lamb. ²⁰ He was foreknown before the foundation of the world but was revealed in these last times for you. ²¹ Through him you believe in God, who raised him from the dead and gave him glory, so that your faith and hope are in God.

_____ / _____ / _____

DATE

²² Since you have purified yourselves by your obedience to the truth, so that you show sincere brotherly love for each other, from a pure heart love one another constantly, ²³ because you have been born again—not of perishable seed but of imperishable—through the living and enduring word of God. ²⁴ For

> All flesh is like grass,
> and all its glory like a flower of the grass.
> The grass withers, and the flower falls,
> ²⁵ but the word of the Lord endures forever.

And this word is the gospel that was proclaimed to you.

him. ⁵ He predestined us to be adopted as sons through Jesus Christ for himself, according to the good pleasure of his will, ⁶ to the praise of his glorious grace that he lavished on us in the Beloved One.

⁷ In him we have redemption through his blood, the forgiveness of our trespasses, according to the riches of his grace ⁸ that he richly poured out on us with all wisdom and understanding. ⁹ He made known to us the mystery of his will, according to his good pleasure that he purposed in Christ ¹⁰ as a plan for the right time—to bring everything together in Christ, both things in heaven and things on earth in him.

ISAIAH 53:7-9

⁷ He was oppressed and afflicted,
yet he did not open his mouth.
Like a lamb led to the slaughter
and like a sheep silent before her shearers,
he did not open his mouth.
⁸ He was taken away because of oppression
     and judgment;
and who considered his fate?
For he was cut off from the land of the living;
he was struck because of my people's rebellion.
⁹ He was assigned a grave with the wicked,
but he was with a rich man at his death,
because he had done no violence
and had not spoken deceitfully.

EPHESIANS 1:3-10

GOD'S RICH BLESSINGS

³ Blessed is the God and Father of our Lord Jesus Christ, who has blessed us with every spiritual blessing in the heavens in Christ. ⁴ For he chose us in him, before the foundation of the world, to be holy and blameless in love before

QUESTIONS

———

What did you notice about this passage?

What questions do you have?

How will you respond?

THE PEOPLE OF GOD

In the opening chapters of 1 Peter, Peter applies Old Testament images of Israel to Gentile Christians, affirming their new identity as the people of God. By describing these believers with phrases from the Old Testament, Peter connects the story of Christians to the broader narrative of God's chosen family. Here's a look at some of these images.

PEOPLE OF GOD

SAVED FROM CAPTIVITY

COVENANT PEOPLE

THE NEW TEMPLE

COVERED BY SACRIFICE

CALLED TO HOLINESS AS A KINGDOM OF PRIESTS

OLD TESTAMENT REFERENCE	APPLIED TO BELIEVERS

CHOSEN BY GOD

Dt 4:37; Is 45:4	To those chosen… **1:1**
Hs 1:9–10; 2:23	…now you are God's people… **2:10**
Ex 34:9; Dt 7:6; 10:15; Ps 33:12; Is 43:20–21	But you are a chosen race…a people for his possession… **2:9**

SAVED FROM CAPTIVITY

Ex 12–15	…you were redeemed from your empty way of life… **1:18**

COVENANT PEOPLE

Is 40; Jr 31	Since you have purified yourselves by your obedience to the truth…because you have been born again—not of perishable seed but of imperishable—through the living and enduring word of God. **1:22–23**

THE NEW TEMPLE

Ps 118:22; Is 28:16	…you yourselves, as living stones, a spiritual house, are being built… **2:5**

COVERED BY SACRIFICE

Ex 24:3–8; Is 52:15	…sprinkled with the blood of Jesus Christ. **1:2**
Ex 12:5; Lv 22:19–25; 23:12; Nm 6:14	…you were redeemed…with the precious blood of Christ, like that of an unblemished and spotless lamb. **1:18–19**

CALLED TO HOLINESS AS A KINGDOM OF PRIESTS

Lv 19:2; 20:7, 26	But as the one who called you is holy, you also are to be holy in all your conduct… **1:15–16**
Ex 19:5–6; 23:22; Is 61:6	But you are…a royal priesthood, a holy nation…so that you may proclaim the praises of the one who called you… **2:9**
Dt 4:20; 7:6; 14:2; Is 43:20–21	…you yourselves…are being built to be a holy priesthood to offer spiritual sacrifices… **2:5**

3

A HOLY PEOPLE

1 Peter 2:1-10
Psalm 34:1-14
Hebrews 13:14-16

1 PETER 2:1-10

THE LIVING STONE AND A HOLY PEOPLE

[1] Therefore, rid yourselves of all malice, all deceit, hypocrisy, envy, and all slander. [2] Like newborn infants, desire the pure milk of the word, so that you may grow up into your salvation, [3] if you have tasted that the Lord is good. [4] As you come to him, a living stone—rejected by people but chosen and honored by God— [5] you yourselves, as living stones, a spiritual house, are being built to be a holy priesthood to offer spiritual sacrifices acceptable to God through Jesus Christ. [6] For it stands in Scripture:

See, I lay a stone in Zion,
a chosen and honored cornerstone,
and the one who believes in him
will never be put to shame.

___/___/___

DATE

[7] So honor will come to you who believe; but for the unbelieving,

> The stone that the builders rejected—
> this one has become the cornerstone,

[8] and

> A stone to stumble over,
> and a rock to trip over.

They stumble because they disobey the word; they were destined for this.

[9] But you are a chosen race, a royal priesthood, a holy nation, a people for his possession, so that you may proclaim the praises of the one who called you out of darkness into his marvelous light. [10] Once you were not a people, but now you are God's people; you had not received mercy, but now you have received mercy.

PSALM 34:1-14

THE LORD DELIVERS THE RIGHTEOUS

Concerning David, when he pretended to be insane in the presence of Abimelech, who drove him out, and he departed.

[1] I will bless the LORD at all times;
his praise will always be on my lips.
[2] I will boast in the LORD;
the humble will hear and be glad.
[3] Proclaim the LORD's greatness with me;
let us exalt his name together.

[4] I sought the LORD, and he answered me
and rescued me from all my fears.
[5] Those who look to him are radiant with joy;
their faces will never be ashamed.
[6] This poor man cried, and the LORD heard him
and saved him from all his troubles.
[7] The angel of the LORD encamps
around those who fear him, and rescues them.

[8] Taste and see that the LORD is good.
How happy is the person who takes refuge in him!
[9] You who are his holy ones, fear the LORD,
for those who fear him lack nothing.
[10] Young lions lack food and go hungry,
but those who seek the LORD
will not lack any good thing.

[11] Come, children, listen to me;
I will teach you the fear of the LORD.
[12] Who is someone who desires life,
loving a long life to enjoy what is good?
[13] Keep your tongue from evil
and your lips from deceitful speech.
[14] Turn away from evil and do what is good;
seek peace and pursue it.

HEBREWS 13:14-16

[14] For we do not have an enduring city here; instead, we seek the one to come. [15] Therefore, through him let us continually offer up to God a sacrifice of praise, that is, the fruit of lips that confess his name. [16] Don't neglect to do what is good and to share, for God is pleased with such sacrifices.

QUESTIONS

———

What did you notice about this passage?

What questions do you have?

How will you respond?

4

A CALL TO
GOOD WORKS

1 Peter 2:11-25
Romans 13:1-7
Galatians 5:13-14

1 PETER 2:11–25

A CALL TO GOOD WORKS

[11] Dear friends, I urge you as strangers and exiles to abstain from sinful desires that wage war against the soul. [12] Conduct yourselves honorably among the Gentiles, so that when they slander you as evildoers, they will observe your good works and will glorify God on the day he visits.

[13] Submit to every human authority because of the Lord, whether to the emperor as the supreme authority [14] or to governors as those sent out by him to punish those who do what is evil and to praise those who do what is good. [15] For it is God's will that you silence the ignorance of foolish people by doing good. [16] Submit as free people, not using your freedom as a cover-up for evil, but as God's slaves. [17] Honor everyone. Love the brothers and sisters. Fear God. Honor the emperor.

SUBMISSION OF SLAVES TO MASTERS

[18] Household slaves, submit to your masters with all reverence not only to the good and gentle ones but also to the cruel. [19] For it brings favor if,

_____/_____/_____

DATE

because of a consciousness of God, someone endures grief from suffering unjustly. [20] For what credit is there if when you do wrong and are beaten, you endure it? But when you do what is good and suffer, if you endure it, this brings favor with God.

[21] For you were called to this, because Christ also suffered for you, leaving you an example, that you should follow in his steps. [22] He did not commit sin, and no deceit was found in his mouth; [23] when he was insulted, he did not insult in return; when he suffered, he did not threaten but entrusted himself to the one who judges justly. [24] He himself bore our sins in his body on the tree; so that, having died to sins, we might live for righteousness. By his wounds you have been healed. [25] For you were like sheep going astray, but you have now returned to the Shepherd and Overseer of your souls.

ROMANS 13:1-7

A CHRISTIAN'S DUTIES TO THE STATE

[1] Let everyone submit to the governing authorities, since there is no authority except from God, and the authorities that exist are instituted by God. [2] So then, the one who resists the authority is opposing God's command, and those who oppose it will bring judgment on themselves. [3] For rulers are not a terror to good conduct, but to bad. Do you want to be unafraid of the authority? Do what is good, and you will have its approval. [4] For it is God's servant for your good. But if you do wrong, be afraid, because it does not carry the sword for no reason. For it is God's servant, an avenger that brings wrath on the one who does wrong. [5] Therefore, you must submit, not only because of wrath but also because of your conscience. [6] And for this reason you pay taxes, since the authorities are God's servants, continually attending to these tasks. [7] Pay your obligations to everyone: taxes to those you owe taxes, tolls to those you owe tolls, respect to those you owe respect, and honor to those you owe honor.

GALATIANS 5:13-14

[13] For you were called to be free, brothers and sisters; only don't use this freedom as an opportunity for the flesh, but serve one another through love. [14] For the whole law is fulfilled in one statement: Love your neighbor as yourself.

QUESTIONS
———————

What did you notice about this passage?

What questions do you have?

How will you respond?

**DON'T LET YOUR BEAUTY CONSIST
OF OUTWARD THINGS...BUT RATHER
WHAT IS INSIDE THE HEART.**

1 PETER 3:2–3

5
―――

WIVES AND HUSBANDS

1 Peter 3:1-7
Genesis 1:26-28
Ephesians 5:22-33

1 PETER 3:1-7

WIVES AND HUSBANDS

[1] In the same way, wives, submit yourselves to your own husbands so that, even if some disobey the word, they may be won over without a word by the way their wives live [2] when they observe your pure, reverent lives. [3] Don't let your beauty consist of outward things like elaborate hairstyles and wearing gold jewelry or fine clothes, [4] but rather what is inside the heart—the imperishable quality of a gentle and quiet spirit, which is of great worth in God's sight. [5] For in the past, the holy women who put their hope in God also adorned themselves in this way, submitting to their own husbands, [6] just as Sarah obeyed Abraham, calling him lord. You have become her children when you do what is good and do not fear any intimidation.

[7] Husbands, in the same way, live with your wives in an understanding way, as with a weaker partner, showing them honor as coheirs of the grace of life, so that your prayers will not be hindered.

_____/_____/_____

DATE

GENESIS 1:26–28

²⁶ Then God said, "Let us make man in our image, according to our likeness. They will rule the fish of the sea, the birds of the sky, the livestock, the whole earth, and the creatures that crawl on the earth."

²⁷ So God created man
in his own image;
he created him in the image of God;
he created them male and female.

²⁸ God blessed them, and God said to them, "Be fruitful, multiply, fill the earth, and subdue it. Rule the fish of the sea, the birds of the sky, and every creature that crawls on the earth."

EPHESIANS 5:22–33

WIVES AND HUSBANDS

²² Wives, submit to your husbands as to the Lord, ²³ because the husband is the head of the wife as Christ is the head of the church. He is the Savior of the body. ²⁴ Now as the church submits to Christ, so also wives are to submit to their husbands in everything. ²⁵ Husbands, love your wives, just as Christ loved the church and gave himself for her ²⁶ to make her holy, cleansing her with the washing of water by the word. ²⁷ He did this to present the church to himself in splendor, without spot or wrinkle or anything like that, but holy and blameless. ²⁸ In the same way, husbands are to love their wives as their own bodies. He who loves his wife loves himself. ²⁹ For no one ever hates his own flesh but provides and cares for it, just as Christ does for the church, ³⁰ since we are members of his body. ³¹ For this reason a man will leave his father and mother and be joined to his wife, and the two will become one flesh. ³² This mystery is profound, but I am talking about Christ and the church. ³³ To sum up, each one of you is to love his wife as himself, and the wife is to respect her husband.

QUESTIONS

———

What did you notice about this passage?

What questions do you have?

How will you respond?

GRACE DAY

Use this day to pray, rest, and reflect on this week's reading,
giving thanks for the grace that is ours in Christ.

———

Galatians 5:13-14

FOR YOU WERE CALLED TO BE FREE,
BROTHERS AND SISTERS; ONLY DON'T USE
THIS FREEDOM AS AN OPPORTUNITY FOR
THE FLESH, BUT SERVE ONE ANOTHER
THROUGH LOVE. FOR THE WHOLE LAW
IS FULFILLED IN ONE STATEMENT:
LOVE YOUR NEIGHBOR AS YOURSELF.

____ / ____ / ____

DATE

7

WEEKLY TRUTH

Scripture is God-breathed and true. When we memorize it,
we carry the gospel with us wherever we go.

This week we will memorize the first part of the key verse
for 1 Peter.

———

———————————

1 Peter 1:3-4

BLESSED BE THE GOD AND FATHER OF
OUR LORD JESUS CHRIST. BECAUSE OF
HIS GREAT MERCY HE HAS GIVEN US NEW
BIRTH INTO A LIVING HOPE THROUGH THE
RESURRECTION OF JESUS CHRIST FROM
THE DEAD AND INTO AN INHERITANCE
THAT IS IMPERISHABLE, UNDEFILED, AND
UNFADING, KEPT IN HEAVEN FOR YOU.

_____/_____/_____

DATE

8

DO NO EVIL

1 PETER 3:8-22

1 Peter 3:8-22
John 15:18-21
Galatians 3:23-29

DO NO EVIL

[8] Finally, all of you be like-minded and sympathetic, love one another, and be compassionate and humble, [9] not paying back evil for evil or insult for insult but, on the contrary, giving a blessing, since you were called for this, so that you may inherit a blessing.

[10] For the one who wants to love life
and to see good days,
let him keep his tongue from evil
and his lips from speaking deceit,
[11] and let him turn away from evil
and do what is good.
Let him seek peace and pursue it,
[12] because the eyes of the Lord are on the righteous
and his ears are open to their prayer.

_____/_____/_____

DATE

But the face of the Lord is against
those who do what is evil.

UNDESERVED SUFFERING

[13] Who then will harm you if you are devoted to what is good? [14] But
even if you should suffer for righteousness, you are blessed. Do not fear
what they fearor be intimidated, [15] but in your hearts regard Christ the
Lord as holy, ready at any time to give a defense to anyone who asks you
for a reason for the hope that is in you. [16] Yet do this with gentleness and
respect, keeping a clear conscience, so that when you are accused, those
who disparage your good conduct in Christ will be put to shame. [17] For
it is better to suffer for doing good, if that should be God's will, than for
doing evil.

[18] For Christ also suffered for sins once for all, the righteous for the
unrighteous, that he might bring you to God. He was put to death in
the flesh but made alive by the Spirit, [19] in which he also went and made
proclamation to the spirits in prison [20] who in the past were disobedient,
when God patiently waited in the days of Noah while the ark was being
prepared. In it a few—that is, eight people—were saved through water.
[21] Baptism, which corresponds to this, now saves you (not as the removal
of dirt from the body, but the pledge of a good conscience toward God)
through the resurrection of Jesus Christ, [22] who has gone into heaven and
is at the right hand of God with angels, authorities, and powers subject
to him.

JOHN 15:18–21

PERSECUTIONS PREDICTED

[18] "If the world hates you, understand that it hated me before it hated
you. [19] If you were of the world, the world would love you as its own.
However, because you are not of the world, but I have chosen you out
of it, the world hates you. [20] Remember the word I spoke to you: 'A
servant is not greater than his master.' If they persecuted me, they will
also persecute you. If they kept my word, they will also keep yours. [21] But
they will do all these things to you on account of my name, because they
don't know the one who sent me."

GALATIANS 3:23-29

[23] Before this faith came, we were confined under the law, imprisoned until the coming faith was revealed. [24] The law, then, was our guardian until Christ, so that we could be justified by faith. [25] But since that faith has come, we are no longer under a guardian, [26] for through faith you are all sons of God in Christ Jesus.

SONS AND HEIRS

[27] For those of you who were baptized into Christ have been clothed with Christ. [28] There is no Jew or Greek, slave or free, male and female; since you are all one in Christ Jesus. [29] And if you belong to Christ, then you are Abraham's seed, heirs according to the promise.

QUESTIONS
———

What did you notice about this passage?

What questions do you have?

How will you respond?

ABOVE ALL, MAINTAIN CONSTANT
LOVE FOR ONE ANOTHER, SINCE
LOVE COVERS A MULTITUDE OF SINS.

1 PETER 4:8

9

FOLLOWING CHRIST

1 Peter 4:1-11
Proverbs 10:12
Romans 6:1-11

1 PETER 4:1-11

FOLLOWING CHRIST

¹ Therefore, since Christ suffered in the flesh, arm yourselves also with the same understanding—because the one who suffers in the flesh is finished with sin— ² in order to live the remaining time in the flesh no longer for human desires, but for God's will. ³ For there has already been enough time spent in doing what the Gentiles choose to do: carrying on in unrestrained behavior, evil desires, drunkenness, orgies, carousing, and lawless idolatry. ⁴ They are surprised that you don't join them in the same flood of wild living—and they slander you. ⁵ They will give an account to the one who stands ready to judge the living and the dead. ⁶ For this reason the gospel was also preached to those who are now dead, so that, although they might be judged in the flesh according to human standards, they might live in the spirit according to God's standards.

END-TIME ETHICS

⁷ The end of all things is near; therefore, be alert and sober-minded for prayer. ⁸ Above all, maintain constant love for one another, since

_____/_____/_____

DATE

love covers a multitude of sins. [9] Be hospitable to one another without complaining. [10] Just as each one has received a gift, use it to serve others, as good stewards of the varied grace of God. [11] If anyone speaks, let it be as one who speaks God's words; if anyone serves, let it be from the strength God provides, so that God may be glorified through Jesus Christ in everything. To him be the glory and the power forever and ever. Amen.

PROVERBS 10:12

Hatred stirs up conflicts,
but love covers all offenses.

ROMANS 6:1-11

THE NEW LIFE IN CHRIST

[1] What should we say then? Should we continue in sin so that grace may multiply? [2] Absolutely not! How can we who died to sin still live in it? [3] Or are you unaware that all of us who were baptized into Christ Jesus were baptized into his death? [4] Therefore we were buried with him by baptism into death, in order that, just as Christ was raised from the dead by the glory of the Father, so we too may walk in newness of life. [5] For if we have been united with him in the likeness of his death, we will certainly also be in the likeness of his resurrection. [6] For we know that our old self was crucified with him so that the body ruled by sin might be rendered powerless so that we may no longer be enslaved to sin, [7] since a person who has died is freed from sin. [8] Now if we died with Christ, we believe that we will also live with him, [9] because we know that Christ, having been raised from the dead, will not die again. Death no longer rules over him. [10] For the death he died, he died to sin once for all time; but the life he lives, he lives to God. [11] So, you too consider yourselves dead to sin and alive to God in Christ Jesus.

QUESTIONS
_____

What did you notice about this passage?

What questions do you have?

How will you respond?

ROME

Adriatic Sea

ACHAIA

CORINTH

Mediterranean Sea

MALTA

N

| 0 MI | | 100 | | 200 | | 300 |
| 0 KM | 100 | 200 | 300 | 400 | |

PETER'S MINISTRY

(A) JERUSALEM
Peter appeals on behalf of Gentile Christians at the Jerusalem Council. **AC 15:6–11**

(B) ANTIOCH
Paul confronts Peter's hypocrisy in Antioch. **GL 2:7–16**

Black Sea

BITHYNIA AND PONTUS

PHRYGIA

GALATIA

CAPPADOCIA

C
ASIA MINOR

CILCIA

PAMPHYLIA

B
ANTIOCH

LYCIA

CYPRUS

SYRIA

A
JERUSALEM

C ASIA MINOR
From Rome, Peter writes to believers who have been scattered across Asia Minor. **1PT 1:1**

E ROME
Peter leads the church in Rome and is later martyred by Nero.

D CORINTH
Peter preaches and ministers in Corinth.
1CO 1:12; 9:5

10

CHRISTIAN SUFFERING

1 Peter 4:12-19
Isaiah 11:1-5
Matthew 5:3-12

1 PETER 4:12-19

CHRISTIAN SUFFERING

¹² Dear friends, don't be surprised when the fiery ordeal comes among you to test you as if something unusual were happening to you. ¹³ Instead, rejoice as you share in the sufferings of Christ, so that you may also rejoice with great joy when his glory is revealed. ¹⁴ If you are ridiculed for the name of Christ, you are blessed, because the Spirit of glory and of God rests on you. ¹⁵ Let none of you suffer as a murderer, a thief, an evildoer, or a meddler. ¹⁶ But if anyone suffers as a Christian, let him not be ashamed but let him glorify God in having that name. ¹⁷ For the time has come for judgment to begin with God's household, and if it begins with us, what will the outcome be for those who disobey the gospel of God?

¹⁸ And if a righteous person is saved with difficulty,
what will become of the ungodly and the sinner?

———— / ————— / —————

DATE

[19] So then, let those who suffer according to God's will entrust themselves to a faithful Creator while doing what is good.

ISAIAH 11:1-5

REIGN OF THE DAVIDIC KING

[1] Then a shoot will grow from the stump
  of Jesse,
and a branch from his roots will bear fruit.
[2] The Spirit of the LORD will rest on him—
a Spirit of wisdom and understanding,
a Spirit of counsel and strength,
a Spirit of knowledge and of the fear of
  the LORD.
[3] His delight will be in the fear of the LORD.
He will not judge
by what he sees with his eyes,
he will not execute justice
by what he hears with his ears,
[4] but he will judge the poor righteously
and execute justice for the oppressed of
  the land.
He will strike the land
with a scepter from his mouth,
and he will kill the wicked
with a command from his lips.
[5] Righteousness will be a belt around his hips;
faithfulness will be a belt around his waist.

MATTHEW 5:3-12

THE BEATITUDES

[3] "Blessed are the poor in spirit,
  for the kingdom of heaven is theirs.
[4] Blessed are those who mourn,
  for they will be comforted.
[5] Blessed are the humble,
  for they will inherit the earth.

[6] Blessed are those who hunger and thirst
for righteousness,
for they will be filled.
[7] Blessed are the merciful,
for they will be shown mercy.
[8] Blessed are the pure in heart,
for they will see God.
[9] Blessed are the peacemakers,
for they will be called sons of God.
[10] Blessed are those who are persecuted
because of righteousness,
for the kingdom of heaven is theirs.

[11] "You are blessed when they insult you and persecute you and falsely say every kind of evil against you because of me. [12] Be glad and rejoice, because your reward is great in heaven. For that is how they persecuted the prophets who were before you."

QUESTIONS

What did you notice about this passage?

What questions do you have?

How will you respond?

ALL OF YOU CLOTHE YOURSELVES WITH
HUMILITY TOWARD ONE ANOTHER...

1 PETER 5:5

11

ABOUT THE ELDERS

1 Peter 5:1-7
Proverbs 3:27-35
1 Timothy 3:1-13

1 PETER 5:1-7

ABOUT THE ELDERS

[1] I exhort the elders among you as a fellow elder and witness to the sufferings of Christ, as well as one who shares in the glory about to be revealed: [2] Shepherd God's flock among you, not overseeing out of compulsion but willingly, as God would have you; not out of greed for money but eagerly; [3] not lording it over those entrusted to you, but being examples to the flock. [4] And when the chief Shepherd appears, you will receive the unfading crown of glory. [5] In the same way, you who are younger, be subject to the elders. All of you clothe yourselves with humility toward one another, because

> God resists the proud
> but gives grace to the humble.

CONCLUSION

[6] Humble yourselves, therefore, under the mighty hand of God, so that he may exalt you at the proper time, [7] casting all your cares on him, because he cares about you.

_____ / _____ / _____

DATE

PROVERBS 3:27-35

TREAT OTHERS FAIRLY

²⁷ When it is in your power,
don't withhold good from the one to whom
    it belongs.
²⁸ Don't say to your neighbor, "Go away!
    Come back later.
I'll give it tomorrow"—when it is there
    with you.
²⁹ Don't plan any harm against your neighbor,
for he trusts you and lives near you.
³⁰ Don't accuse anyone without cause,
when he has done you no harm.
³¹ Don't envy a violent man
or choose any of his ways;
³² for the devious are detestable to the LORD,
but he is a friend to the upright.
³³ The LORD's curse is on the household of
    the wicked,
but he blesses the home of the righteous;
³⁴ He mocks those who mock,
but gives grace to the humble.
³⁵ The wise will inherit honor,
but he holds up fools to dishonor.

1 TIMOTHY 3:1-13

QUALIFICATIONS FOR OVERSEERS
AND DEACONS

¹ This saying is trustworthy: "If anyone aspires to be an overseer, he desires a noble work." ² An overseer, therefore, must be above reproach, the husband of one wife, self-controlled, sensible, respectable, hospitable, able to teach, ³ not an excessive drinker, not a bully but gentle, not quarrelsome, not greedy. ⁴ He must manage his own household competently and have his children under control with all dignity. ⁵ (If anyone does not know how to manage his own household, how will he take care of God's church?) ⁶ He must not be a new convert, or he might become conceited and incur the same condemnation as the devil. ⁷ Furthermore, he must have a good reputation among outsiders, so that he does not fall into disgrace and the devil's trap.

⁸ Deacons, likewise, should be worthy of respect, not hypocritical, not drinking a lot of wine, not greedy for money, ⁹ holding the mystery of the faith with a clear conscience. ¹⁰ They must also be tested first; if they prove blameless, then they can serve as deacons. ¹¹ Wives, too, must be worthy of respect, not slanderers, self-controlled, faithful in everything. ¹² Deacons are to be husbands of one wife, managing their children and their own households competently. ¹³ For those who have served well as deacons acquire a good standing for themselves and great boldness in the faith that is in Christ Jesus.

QUESTIONS

———

What did you notice about this passage?

What questions do you have?

How will you respond?

FIRM IN THE FAITH

1 Peter 5:8-14
2 Corinthians 4:7-18
Ephesians 6:12-20

1 PETER 5:8-14

8 Be sober-minded, be alert. Your adversary the devil is prowling around like a roaring lion, looking for anyone he can devour. 9 Resist him, firm in the faith, knowing that the same kind of sufferings are being experienced by your fellow believers throughout the world.

10 The God of all grace, who called you to his eternal glory in Christ, will himself restore, establish, strengthen, and support you after you have suffered a little while. 11 To him be dominion forever. Amen.

12 Through Silvanus, a faithful brother (as I consider him), I have written to you briefly in order to encourage you and to testify that this is the true grace of God. Stand firm in it! 13 She who is in Babylon, chosen together with you, sends you greetings, as does Mark, my son. 14 Greet one another with a kiss of love. Peace to all of you who are in Christ.

———/———/———

DATE

2 CORINTHIANS 4:7-18

TREASURE IN CLAY JARS

[7] Now we have this treasure in clay jars, so that this extraordinary power may be from God and not from us. [8] We are afflicted in every way but not crushed; we are perplexed but not in despair; [9] we are persecuted but not abandoned; we are struck down but not destroyed. [10] We always carry the death of Jesus in our body, so that the life of Jesus may also be displayed in our body. [11] For we who live are always being given over to death for Jesus's sake, so that Jesus's life may also be displayed in our mortal flesh. [12] So then, death is at work in us, but life in you. [13] And since we have the same spirit of faith in keeping with what is written, I believed, therefore I spoke, we also believe, and therefore speak. [14] For we know that the one who raised the Lord Jesus will also raise us with Jesus and present us with you. [15] Indeed, everything is for your benefit so that, as grace extends through more and more people, it may cause thanksgiving to increase to the glory of God.

[16] Therefore we do not give up. Even though our outer person is being destroyed, our inner person is being renewed day by day. [17] For our momentary light affliction is producing for us an absolutely incomparable eternal weight of glory. [18] So we do not focus on what is seen, but on what is unseen. For what is seen is temporary, but what is unseen is eternal.

EPHESIANS 6:12-20

[12] For our struggle is not against flesh and blood, but against the rulers, against the authorities, against the cosmic powers of this darkness, against evil, spiritual forces in the heavens. [13] For this reason take up the full armor of God, so that you may be able to resist in the evil day, and having prepared everything, to take your stand. [14] Stand, therefore, with truth like a belt around your waist, righteousness like armor on your chest, [15] and your feet sandaled with readiness for the gospel of peace. [16] In every situation take up the shield of faith with which you can extinguish all the flaming arrows of the evil one. [17] Take the helmet of salvation and the sword of the Spirit—which is the word of God. [18] Pray at all times in the Spirit with every prayer and request, and stay alert with all perseverance and intercession for all the saints. [19] Pray also for me, that the message may be given to me when I open my mouth to make known with boldness the mystery of the gospel. [20] For this I am an ambassador in chains. Pray that I might be bold enough to speak about it as I should.

QUESTIONS
————

What did you notice about this passage?

What questions do you have?

How will you respond?

GRACE DAY

Use this day to pray, rest, and reflect on this week's reading,
giving thanks for the grace that is ours in Christ.

Galatians 3:27-29

FOR THOSE OF YOU WHO WERE
BAPTIZED INTO CHRIST HAVE BEEN
CLOTHED WITH CHRIST. THERE IS NO JEW
OR GREEK, SLAVE OR FREE, MALE AND
FEMALE; SINCE YOU ARE ALL ONE IN
CHRIST JESUS. AND IF YOU BELONG TO
CHRIST, THEN YOU ARE ABRAHAM'S SEED,
HEIRS ACCORDING TO THE PROMISE.

_____ / _____ / _____

DATE

14

WEEKLY TRUTH

Scripture is God-breathed and true. When we memorize it,
we carry the gospel with us wherever we go.

This week we will memorize the second part of the
key verse for 1 Peter.

———————

1 Peter 1:3-4

BLESSED BE THE GOD AND FATHER OF
OUR LORD JESUS CHRIST. BECAUSE OF
HIS GREAT MERCY HE HAS GIVEN US NEW
BIRTH INTO A LIVING HOPE THROUGH THE
RESURRECTION OF JESUS CHRIST FROM
THE DEAD AND INTO AN INHERITANCE
THAT IS IMPERISHABLE, UNDEFILED, AND
UNFADING, KEPT IN HEAVEN FOR YOU.

_____ / _____ / _____

DATE

KEY VERSE
2 PETER 1:3

His divine power has given us everything required for life and godliness through the knowledge of him who called us by his own glory and goodness.

ON THE TIMELINE

Second Peter was written just before Peter's death, as indicated by his mention in 1:14 that his death was near. Peter likely wrote the letter from Rome, where Church tradition places the apostle in his latter days. Peter's martyrdom occurred around AD 66, during Nero's reign.

A LITTLE BACKGROUND

The author of 2 Peter plainly identified himself as the apostle Peter, calling himself "Simeon Peter" (1:1), a name only used of the apostle one other time in Scripture, in Acts 15:14. The Semitic spelling of the name lends a sense of authenticity to Peter's letter, and it would have been natural for Peter, as a Jew, to use this original form of his name. Peter designated himself as "a servant and an apostle of Jesus Christ" (1:1). He saw himself as a servant submitted to Christ's lordship and as a divinely ordained, directly commissioned, authoritative representative of the Lord Jesus Himself.

Unlike 1 Peter, 2 Peter does not mention specific recipients or an exact destination. The apostle referred to his epistle as the "second letter" he had written to his readers (3:1).

MESSAGE & PURPOSE

Peter cautioned believers to beware of false teachers with their heretical doctrines and immoral lifestyles. Peter was so concerned about the temptations of sin that he wrote this second letter as an immediate follow-up to the first. Peter also warned against denials of Christ's return and His accompanying judgment. He urged his readers to make every effort to grow in the knowledge and practice of the Christian faith.

GIVE THANKS FOR THE BOOK OF 2 PETER

The Word of God is preeminent in this short letter. Second Peter gives Scripture center stage in chapter 1 by emphasizing knowledge (1:3, 5, 6, 8, 12, 20–21) and its divine origin; in chapter 2 by showing its historicity (2:4–8); and in chapter 3 by indicating Paul's letters are equal with "the rest of the Scriptures" (3:15–16). Peter made strong connections with the Old Testament and challenged his audience to live authentic Christian lives, insisting on the importance of Scripture for guiding and preserving our faith.

**MAY GRACE AND PEACE BE MULTIPLIED
TO YOU THROUGH THE KNOWLEDGE OF
GOD AND OF JESUS OUR LORD.**

2 PETER 1:2

15

GROWTH IN THE FAITH

2 Peter 1:1-15
John 21:17-19
Titus 3:4-7

2 PETER 1:1–15

GREETING

¹ Simeon Peter, a servant and an apostle of Jesus Christ:

To those who have received a faith equal to ours through the righteousness of our God and Savior Jesus Christ.

² May grace and peace be multiplied to you through the knowledge of God and of Jesus our Lord.

GROWTH IN THE FAITH

³ His divine power has given us everything required for life and godliness through the knowledge of him who called us by his own glory and goodness. ⁴ By these he has given us very great and precious promises, so that through them you may share in the divine nature, escaping the corruption that is in the world because of evil desire. ⁵ For this very

_____/_____/_____

DATE

reason, make every effort to supplement your faith with goodness, goodness with knowledge, [6] knowledge with self-control, self-control with endurance, endurance with godliness, [7] godliness with brotherly affection, and brotherly affection with love. [8] For if you possess these qualities in increasing measure, they will keep you from being useless or unfruitful in the knowledge of our Lord Jesus Christ. [9] The person who lacks these things is blind and shortsighted and has forgotten the cleansing from his past sins. [10] Therefore, brothers and sisters, make every effort to confirm your calling and election, because if you do these things you will never stumble. [11] For in this way, entry into the eternal kingdom of our Lord and Savior Jesus Christ will be richly provided for you.

[12] Therefore I will always remind you about these things, even though you know them and are established in the truth you now have. [13] I think it is right, as long as I am in this bodily tent, to wake you up with a reminder, [14] since I know that I will soon lay aside my tent, as our Lord Jesus Christ has indeed made clear to me. [15] And I will also make every effort so that you are able to recall these things at any time after my departure.

JOHN 21:17-19

[17] He asked him the third time, "Simon, son of John, do you love me?"

Peter was grieved that he asked him the third time, "Do you love me?" He said, "Lord, you know everything; you know that I love you."

"Feed my sheep," Jesus said. [18] "Truly I tell you, when you were younger, you would tie your belt and walk wherever you wanted. But when you grow old, you will stretch out your hands and someone else will tie you and carry you where you don't want to go." [19] He said this to indicate by what kind of death Peter would glorify God. After saying this, he told him, "Follow me."

TITUS 3:4-7

[4] But when the kindness of God our Savior and his love for mankind appeared, [5] he saved us—not by works of righteousness that we had done, but according to his mercy—through the washing of regeneration and renewal by the Holy Spirit. [6] He poured out his Spirit on us abundantly through Jesus Christ our Savior [7] so that, having been justified by his grace, we may become heirs with the hope of eternal life.

QUESTIONS
———

What did you notice about this passage?

What questions do you have?

How will you respond?

16

THE TRUSTWORTHY PROPHETIC WORD

2 Peter 1:16–21
Matthew 17:1-8
2 Timothy 3:10-17

2 PETER 1:16–21

THE TRUSTWORTHY PROPHETIC WORD

[16] For we did not follow cleverly contrived myths when we made known to you the power and coming of our Lord Jesus Christ; instead, we were eyewitnesses of his majesty. [17] For he received honor and glory from God the Father when the voice came to him from the Majestic Glory, saying "This is my beloved Son, with whom I am well-pleased!" [18] We ourselves heard this voice when it came from heaven while we were with him on the holy mountain. [19] We also have the prophetic word strongly confirmed, and you will do well to pay attention to it, as to a lamp shining in a dark place, until the day dawns and the morning star rises in your hearts. [20] Above all, you know this: No prophecy of Scripture comes from the prophet's own interpretation, [21] because no prophecy ever came by the will of man; instead, men spoke from God as they were carried along by the Holy Spirit.

_____/_____/_____

DATE

MATTHEW 17:1-8

THE TRANSFIGURATION

¹ After six days Jesus took Peter, James, and his brother John and led them up on a high mountain by themselves. ² He was transfigured in front of them, and his face shone like the sun; his clothes became as white as the light. ³ Suddenly, Moses and Elijah appeared to them, talking with him. ⁴ Then Peter said to Jesus, "Lord, it's good for us to be here. I will set up three shelters here: one for you, one for Moses, and one for Elijah."

⁵ While he was still speaking, suddenly a bright cloud covered them, and a voice from the cloud said: "This is my beloved Son, with whom I am well-pleased. Listen to him!" ⁶ When the disciples heard this, they fell facedown and were terrified.

⁷ Jesus came up, touched them, and said, "Get up; don't be afraid." ⁸ When they looked up they saw no one except Jesus alone.

2 TIMOTHY 3:10-17

STRUGGLES IN THE CHRISTIAN LIFE

¹⁰ But you have followed my teaching, conduct, purpose, faith, patience, love, and endurance, ¹¹ along with the persecutions and sufferings that came to me in Antioch, Iconium, and Lystra. What persecutions I endured—and yet the Lord rescued me from them all. ¹² In fact, all who want to live a godly life in Christ Jesus will be persecuted. ¹³ Evil people and impostors will become worse, deceiving and being deceived. ¹⁴ But as for you, continue in what you have learned and firmly believed. You know those who taught you, ¹⁵ and you know that from infancy you have known the sacred Scriptures, which are able to give you wisdom for salvation through faith in Christ Jesus. ¹⁶ All Scripture is inspired by God and is profitable for teaching, for rebuking, for correcting, for training in righteousness, ¹⁷ so that the man of God may be complete, equipped for every good work.

QUESTIONS
———

What did you notice about this passage?

What questions do you have?

How will you respond?

HERESIES IN HISTORY

False teachings and heresies are nothing new. Peter warned, "There were indeed false prophets among the people, just as there will be false teachers among you" (2Pt 2:1). If left unchecked, false teachings can "shipwreck" the faith of believers who are not anchored in God's Word (1Tm 1:9).

Below is a summary of some of the most influential heresies in Church history. Though each of these movements have long been condemned by Bible-believing Christians, their poisonous impact can still be felt today.

GNOSTICISM

The term *gnosticism* comes from the Greek word for "knowledge," *gnosis*. That's because gnosticism, in its many varieties, is characterized by secret knowledge. Gnostics believed the material world is evil while the spiritual world is good. They also believed human beings contain a divine spark that longs to be set free from the prison of a physical body, and that salvation could be found by learning secret knowledge, rather than through faith.

SEE 1TM 4:1-5; 6:20

MARCIONISM

Seeing God in the Old Testament as full of wrath and vengeance, Marcion postulated that the God of the New Testament, revealed by His Son, Jesus, must be a superior and altogether separate deity. In Marcion thought, Jesus was not actually human, but only appeared in human form (see Docetism). Marcion's "Bible" was made up of portions of Luke's Gospel (collected as the Gospel of Marcion) and ten of Paul's thirteen letters.

SEE JN 10:30; 14:28

DOCETISM

In the broadest of terms, docetism is the belief that Christ only seemed to have a physical body. (Docetism comes from the Greek word *dokein*, "to seem.") As in Marcionism, the idea is that since Christ is God, He could not possibly be contained in a physical body. Therefore, docetism suggests He only seemed human during His earthly life. According to this heresy, what was seen as Jesus's body was actually only an illusion or phantom.

SEE JN 1:14; RM 8:3

MODALISM

Modalism posits that since there is one God, He cannot exist in three persons. Instead, the Father, Son, and the Holy Spirit are three manifestations, or modes, of God. To put this belief another way, Yahweh of the Old Testament became Jesus in the Gospels and later the Holy Spirit who indwells believers. In modalism, there is no real distinction made between God the Father, God the Son, and God the Spirit. They are considered one and the same, not only in essence, but also in person.

SEE MT 28:19; LK 3:21-22

ARIANISM

In the late third century, Arius began teaching that Jesus was a created being and therefore inferior to God the Father. In other words, Arius believed God the Son is not coeternal with God the Father, and there was a time before the Son came into being when the Father existed on His own. According to Arius, God the Father alone is infinite and Jesus was made God by the will and permission of the Father. In addition, he believed the Holy Spirit was created by the Father with the help of the Son and is inferior to both.

SEE JN 1:1-3; COL 1:15-19

PELAGIANISM

Pelagius was a British monk who lived in the late fourth and early fifth centuries AD. According to his teaching, original sin did not so taint the human will that men and women could no longer choose obedience to God. As such, Pelagius and his followers denied the necessity of grace and instead held to a works-based salvation. They also believed that because the human will was created by God, a sinless life was possible.

SEE PS 51:5; RM 3:10-12

DEISM

Popularized during the Enlightenment, deism is a philosophical system that upholds God as Creator of the universe ("the First Cause") but denies that He has had any direct involvement with His creation since. God, in this system, is like a watchmaker who wound the watch (the universe) at the beginning of time and now allows natural processes to run their course unfettered. As a result, deists reject the existence of any divine revelation, including the Bible as the Word of God, and miracles. Instead, they believe reason is sufficient for understanding our world and proving the existence of God.

SEE MT 10:29; HEB 1:1-3

FALSE TEACHING

There is no message more precious or powerful than the gospel of Jesus Christ. That's why, as Paul instructed Timothy, we must guard the faith handed down to us (1Tm 6:20). Below you'll find some of what Jesus, Paul, Peter, John, and Jude had to say on the subject of false teachers. Practical instructions are indicated with bold text.

JESUS

MATTHEW 7:15-20

[15] **"Be on your guard against false prophets who come to you in sheep's clothing but inwardly are ravaging wolves.** [16] You'll recognize them by their fruit. Are grapes gathered from thornbushes or figs from thistles? [17] In the same way, every good tree produces good fruit, but a bad tree produces bad fruit. [18] A good tree can't produce bad fruit; neither can a bad tree produce good fruit. [19] Every tree that doesn't produce good fruit is cut down and thrown into the fire. [20] So you'll recognize them by their fruit."

SEE ALSO MT 15:14

PAUL

ROMANS 16:17-18

[17] **Now I urge you, brothers and sisters, to watch out for those who create divisions and obstacles contrary to the teaching that you learned. Avoid them,** [18] because such people do not serve our Lord Christ but their own appetites. They deceive the hearts of the unsuspecting with smooth talk and flattering words.

SEE ALSO AC 20:29-30; 2CO 11:13-14; GL 1:8-9; EPH 5:6; COL 2:8; 1TM 1:5-7; 4:1-5; 6:3-5; 2TM 3:3-9; 4:3-4; TI 1:10-11, 15-16

PETER

2 PETER 2:1–3

¹ There were indeed false prophets among the people, just as there will be false teachers among you. They will bring in destructive heresies, even denying the Master who bought them, and will bring swift destruction on themselves. ² Many will follow their depraved ways, and the way of truth will be maligned because of them. ³ They will exploit you in their greed with made-up stories. Their condemnation, pronounced long ago, is not idle, and their destruction does not sleep.

JOHN

2 JOHN 8–11

⁸ **Watch yourselves so you don't lose what we have worked for, but that you may receive a full reward.** ⁹ Anyone who does not remain in Christ's teaching but goes beyond it does not have God. The one who remains in that teaching, this one has both the Father and the Son. ¹⁰ **If anyone comes to you and does not bring this teaching, do not receive him into your home, and don't greet him;** ¹¹ for the one who greets him shares in his evil works.

SEE ALSO 1JN 2:18–19, 26–27

JUDE

JUDE 4

For some people, who were designated for this judgment long ago, have come in by stealth; they are ungodly, turning the grace of our God into sensuality and denying Jesus Christ, our only Master and Lord.

THE LORD KNOWS HOW TO
RESCUE THE GODLY FROM TRIALS

2 PETER 2:9

17

THE JUDGMENT OF FALSE TEACHERS

2 Peter 2
John 10:27-29
Ephesians 2:19-22

2 PETER 2

THE JUDGMENT OF FALSE TEACHERS

¹ There were indeed false prophets among the people, just as there will be false teachers among you. They will bring in destructive heresies, even denying the Master who bought them, and will bring swift destruction on themselves. ² Many will follow their depraved ways, and the way of truth will be maligned because of them. ³ They will exploit you in their greed with made-up stories. Their condemnation, pronounced long ago, is not idle, and their destruction does not sleep.

⁴ For if God didn't spare the angels who sinned but cast them into hell and delivered them in chains of utter darkness to be kept for judgment; ⁵ and if he didn't spare the ancient world, but protected Noah, a preacher of righteousness, and seven others, when he brought the flood on the world of the ungodly; ⁶ and if he reduced the cities of Sodom and Gomorrah to ashes and condemned them to extinction, making them

_____/_____/_____

DATE

an example of what is coming to the ungodly; [7] and if he rescued righteous Lot, distressed by the depraved behavior of the immoral [8] (for as that righteous man lived among them day by day, his righteous soul was tormented by the lawless deeds he saw and heard)— [9] then the Lord knows how to rescue the godly from trials and to keep the unrighteous under punishment for the day of judgment, [10] especially those who follow the polluting desires of the flesh and despise authority.

Bold, arrogant people! They are not afraid to slander the glorious ones; [11] however, angels, who are greater in might and power, do not bring a slanderous charge against them before the Lord. [12] But these people, like irrational animals—creatures of instinct born to be caught and destroyed—slander what they do not understand, and in their destruction they too will be destroyed. [13] They will be paid back with harm for the harm they have done. They consider it a pleasure to carouse in broad daylight. They are spots and blemishes, delighting in their deceptions while they feast with you. [14] They have eyes full of adultery that never stop looking for sin. They seduce unstable people and have hearts trained in greed. Children under a curse! [15] They have gone astray by abandoning the straight path and have followed the path of Balaam, the son of Bosor, who loved the wages of wickedness [16] but received a rebuke for his lawlessness: A speechless donkey spoke with a human voice and restrained the prophet's madness.

[17] These people are springs without water, mists driven by a storm. The gloom of darkness has been reserved for them. [18] For by uttering boastful, empty words, they seduce, with fleshly desires and debauchery, people who have barely escaped from those who live in error. [19] They promise them freedom, but they themselves are slaves of corruption, since people are enslaved to whatever defeats them. [20] For if, having escaped the world's impurity through the knowledge of the Lord and Savior Jesus Christ, they are again entangled in these things and defeated, the last state is worse for them than the first. [21] For it would have been better for them not to have known the way of righteousness than, after knowing it, to turn back from the holy command delivered to them. [22] It has happened to them according to the true proverb: A dog returns to its own vomit, and, "A washed sow returns to wallowing in the mud."

JOHN 10:27-29

[27] "My sheep hear my voice, I know them, and they follow me. [28] I give them eternal life, and they will never perish. No one will snatch them out of my hand. [29] My Father, who has given them to me, is greater than all. No one is able to snatch them out of the Father's hand."

EPHESIANS 2:19-22

[19] So then you are no longer foreigners and strangers, but fellow citizens with the saints, and members of God's household, [20] built on the foundation of the apostles and prophets, with Christ Jesus himself as the cornerstone. [21] In him the whole building, being put together, grows into a holy temple in the Lord. [22] In him you are also being built together for God's dwelling in the Spirit.

QUESTIONS
———

What did you notice about this passage?

What questions do you have?

How will you respond?

18

THE DAY OF THE LORD

2 Peter 3:1-13
Genesis 1:6-10; 7:17-24
Revelation 21:1-8

2 PETER 3:1-13

THE DAY OF THE LORD

¹ Dear friends, this is now the second letter I have written to you; in both letters, I want to stir up your sincere understanding by way of reminder, ² so that you recall the words previously spoken by the holy prophets and the command of our Lord and Savior given through your apostles. ³ Above all, be aware of this: Scoffers will come in the last days scoffing and following their own evil desires, ⁴ saying, "Where is his 'coming' that he promised? Ever since our ancestors fell asleep, all things continue as they have been since the beginning of creation." ⁵ They deliberately overlook this: By the word of God the heavens came into being long ago and the earth was brought about from water and through water. ⁶ Through these the world of that time perished when it was flooded. ⁷ By the same word, the present heavens and earth are stored up for fire, being kept for the day of judgment and destruction of the ungodly.

_____/____/_____

DATE

[8] Dear friends, don't overlook this one fact: With the Lord one day is like a thousand years, and a thousand years like one day. [9] The Lord does not delay his promise, as some understand delay, but is patient with you, not wanting any to perish but all to come to repentance.

[10] But the day of the Lord will come like a thief; on that day the heavens will pass away with a loud noise, the elements will burn and be dissolved, and the earth and the works on it will be disclosed. [11] Since all these things are to be dissolved in this way, it is clear what sort of people you should be in holy conduct and godliness [12] as you wait for the day of God and hasten its coming. Because of that day, the heavens will be dissolved with fire and the elements will melt with heat. [13] But based on his promise, we wait for new heavens and a new earth, where righteousness dwells.

GENESIS 1:6-10

[6] Then God said, "Let there be an expanse between the waters, separating water from water." [7] So God made the expanse and separated the water under the expanse from the water above the expanse. And it was so. [8] God called the expanse "sky." Evening came and then morning: the second day.

[9] Then God said, "Let the water under the sky be gathered into one place, and let the dry land appear." And it was so. [10] God called the dry land "earth," and the gathering of the water he called "seas." And God saw that it was good.

GENESIS 7:17-24

[17] The flood continued for forty days on the earth; the water increased and lifted up the ark so that it rose above the earth. [18] The water surged and increased greatly on the earth, and the ark floated on the surface of the water. [19] Then the water surged even higher on the earth, and all the high mountains under the whole sky were covered. [20] The mountains were covered as the water surged above them more than twenty feet. [21] Every creature perished—those that crawl on the earth, birds, livestock, wildlife, and those that swarm on the earth, as well as all mankind. [22] Everything with the breath of the spirit of life in its nostrils—everything on dry land died. [23] He wiped out every living thing that was on the face of the earth, from mankind to livestock, to creatures that crawl, to the

birds of the sky, and they were wiped off the earth. Only Noah was left, and those that were with him in the ark. [24] And the water surged on the earth 150 days.

REVELATION 21:1–8

THE NEW CREATION

[1] Then I saw a new heaven and a new earth; for the first heaven and the first earth had passed away, and the sea was no more. [2] I also saw the holy city, the new Jerusalem, coming down out of heaven from God, prepared like a bride adorned for her husband.

[3] Then I heard a loud voice from the throne: Look, God's dwelling is with humanity, and he will live with them. They will be his peoples, and God himself will be with them and will be their God. [4] He will wipe away every tear from their eyes. Death will be no more; grief, crying, and pain will be no more, because the previous things have passed away.

[5] Then the one seated on the throne said, "Look, I am making everything new." He also said, "Write, because these words are faithful and true." [6] Then he said to me, "It is done! I am the Alpha and the Omega, the beginning and the end. I will freely give to the thirsty from the spring of the water of life. [7] The one who conquers will inherit these things, and I will be his God, and he will be my son. [8] But the cowards, faithless, detestable, murderers, sexually immoral, sorcerers, idolaters, and all liars—their share will be in the lake that burns with fire and sulfur, which is the second death."

QUESTIONS

What did you notice about this passage?

What questions do you have?

How will you respond?

TO HIM BE THE GLORY BOTH NOW AND TO THE DAY OF ETERNITY.

2 PETER 3:18

19

TO HIM BE THE GLORY

2 Peter 3:14-18
2 Corinthians 4:1-6
Galatians 5:1-6

2 PETER 3:14-18

CONCLUSION

¹⁴ Therefore, dear friends, while you wait for these things, make every effort to be found without spot or blemish in his sight, at peace. ¹⁵ Also, regard the patience of our Lord as salvation, just as our dear brother Paul has written to you according to the wisdom given to him. ¹⁶ He speaks about these things in all his letters. There are some matters that are hard to understand. The untaught and unstable will twist them to their own destruction, as they also do with the rest of the Scriptures.

¹⁷ Therefore, dear friends, since you know this in advance, be on your guard, so that you are not led away by the error of lawless people and fall from your own stable position. ¹⁸ But grow in the grace and knowledge of our Lord and Savior Jesus Christ. To him be the glory both now and to the day of eternity.

___ / ___ / ___

DATE

2 CORINTHIANS 4:1-6

THE LIGHT OF THE GOSPEL

[1] Therefore, since we have this ministry because we were shown mercy, we do not give up. [2] Instead, we have renounced secret and shameful things, not acting deceitfully or distorting the word of God, but commending ourselves before God to everyone's conscience by an open display of the truth. [3] But if our gospel is veiled, it is veiled to those who are perishing. [4] In their case, the god of this age has blinded the minds of the unbelievers to keep them from seeing the light of the gospel of the glory of Christ, who is the image of God. [5] For we are not proclaiming ourselves but Jesus Christ as Lord, and ourselves as your servants for Jesus's sake. [6] For God who said, "Let light shine out of darkness," has shone in our hearts to give the light of the knowledge of God's glory in the face of Jesus Christ.

GALATIANS 5:1-6

FREEDOM OF THE CHRISTIAN

[1] For freedom, Christ set us free. Stand firm then and don't submit again to a yoke of slavery. [2] Take note! I, Paul, am telling you that if you get yourselves circumcised, Christ will not benefit you at all. [3] Again I testify to every man who gets himself circumcised that he is obligated to do the entire law. [4] You who are trying to be justified by the law are alienated from Christ; you have fallen from grace. [5] For we eagerly await through the Spirit, by faith, the hope of righteousness. [6] For in Christ Jesus neither circumcision nor uncircumcision accomplishes anything; what matters is faith working through love.

QUESTIONS
————

What did you notice about this passage?

What questions do you have?

How will you respond?

GRACE DAY

Use this day to pray, rest, and reflect on this week's reading, giving thanks for the grace that is ours in Christ.

Ephesians 2:19-22

SO THEN YOU ARE NO LONGER
FOREIGNERS AND STRANGERS, BUT
FELLOW CITIZENS WITH THE SAINTS,
AND MEMBERS OF GOD'S HOUSEHOLD,
BUILT ON THE FOUNDATION OF THE
APOSTLES AND PROPHETS, WITH CHRIST
JESUS HIMSELF AS THE CORNERSTONE.
IN HIM THE WHOLE BUILDING, BEING
PUT TOGETHER, GROWS INTO A HOLY
TEMPLE IN THE LORD. IN HIM YOU ARE
ALSO BEING BUILT TOGETHER FOR GOD'S
DWELLING IN THE SPIRIT.

_____ / _____ / _____

DATE

WEEKLY TRUTH

Scripture is God-breathed and true. When we memorize it,
we carry the gospel with us wherever we go.

This week we will memorize the key verse for 2 Peter.

———

_____

2 Peter 1:3

HIS DIVINE POWER HAS GIVEN US
EVERYTHING REQUIRED FOR LIFE AND
GODLINESS THROUGH THE KNOWLEDGE
OF HIM WHO CALLED US BY HIS OWN
GLORY AND GOODNESS.

_____ / _____ / _____

DATE

MY HOPE IS BUILT ON NOTHING LESS THAN JESUS' BLOOD AND RIGHTEOUS- NESS.

FROM *ON CHRIST THE SOLID ROCK* BY EDWARD MOTE

 **HE READS TRUTH**

MEN IN THE WORD OF GOD EVERY DAY.

He Reads Truth is a community of men who read God's Word together every day. We help men engage with Scripture through daily Bible reading plans, online essays about each day's reading, and printed resources designed for deeper engagement. Start reading along today.

@hereadstruth | hereadstruth.com

Where did I study?

- ☐ HOME
- ☐ OFFICE
- ☐ CHURCH
- ☐ SCHOOL
- ☐ COFFEE SHOP
- ☐ OTHER:

_____

_____

WHAT WAS I LISTENING TO?

Song: _____

Artist: _____

Album: _____

_____

What time of day did I study?

- ☐ MORNING
- ☐ AFTERNOON
- ☐ NIGHT
- ☐ OTHER:

_____

_____

What was happening in the world?

_____

_____

_____

_____

What was happening in my life?

_____

_____

_____

_____

_____

_____

MY CLOSING PRAYER:

_____

END DATE

_____ / _____ / _____